Immortality

Also by Alan Feldman

Poetry Books
The Happy Genius
A Sail to Great Island

Poetry Chapbooks
The Household
Audit/Poetry (vol. 6, no 1)
The Personals
Anniversary
Round Trip
On the Zócalo
The Blue Boat
Beloved Young
Strange Places
Flowers in Wartime

Criticism
Frank O'Hara

Nonfiction
State College 101: A Freshman Writing Class

For Children
Lucy Mastermind

Immortality

Alan Feldman

The University of Wisconsin Press

Publication of this volume has been made possible, in part, through support from the Brittingham Fund.

The University of Wisconsin Press
1930 Monroe Street, 3rd Floor
Madison, Wisconsin 53711-2059
uwpress.wisc.edu

3 Henrietta Street, Covent Garden
London WC2E 8LU, United Kingdom
eurospanbookstore.com

Printed in the United States of America

Library of Congress Cataloging-in-Publication Data

Feldman, Alan, 1945– author.
[Poems. Selections]
Immortality / Alan Feldman.
pages   cm — (Four Lakes poetry series)
ISBN 978-0-299-30334-1 (pbk.: alk. paper)
ISBN 978-0-299-30333-4 (e-book)
I. Title.   II. Series: Four Lakes poetry series.
PS3556.E458A6   2015
811′.54—dc23
2014030774

For
Zoe
and
Abigail

This is what your consciousness has breathed and lived on and enjoyed throughout your life—your soul, your immortality, your life in others. And what now?

—Boris Pasternak, *Dr. Zhivago*

Contents

Acknowledgments

I am grateful to the editors of the publications where these poems first appeared:

Arroyo: "Just Once" and "What the Pig Meant"

Artful Dodge: "The Reason for the Child"

Boston Poetry Magazine: "A Summer Afternoon" and "Oxytocin"

Cortland Review: "Watch Battery"

Catamaran: "The Light"

Cincinnati Review: "A Message from My Mother," "In Response to My Fear That I'll Receive Another Call from the Yacht Salesman"

Cimarron Review: "The Tiny Couple," "House of Refuge," and "Quintet"

Hanging Loose: "When My Book Group Reconvened after So Many Years"

Kenyon Review: "The Blue Boat," "Two Walks," and "Uncontested"

TLR: The Literary Review: "How to Improvise" and "Sincerity and Authenticity"

Ploughshares: "Landlocked" and "My Happiness"

Rabbit Ears: TV Poems: "Fame"

Salamander: "Ashore in Oak Bluffs," "Hate," "The News," "A Little Ode to Television," and "How Big?"

Southern Review: "Flight from Cyprus," "Reading Taha by Lamplight," "The Afterlife," "The Bad Singers of San Miguel de Allende," and "Lunch at the Brew Moon"

Southwest Review: "Imagining Uruguay"

Tiferet: "The Blessing of the Poodles"

upstreet: "In November," "Pathetic, Those Chickadees," "The Terrible Memory," and "Love Poem"

Worcester Review: "To Vocabulary"
Yale Review: "A Walk to the Spring"

"In November" was reprinted in *Best American Poetry 2011*, edited by Kevin Young. "How Big?" appeared on *Poetry Daily* (poems.com) as "poem of the day" on July 15, 2011; "The Afterlife" on November 17, 2013; and "Landlocked" on December 24, 2013. "At the Dentist" won first prize in 2011 at the annual W. B. Yeats Society competition in New York. "Oaxaca" originally appeared in *On the Zócalo*, a chapbook that was privately printed in 2007. The quotations from Taha Muhammad Ali are from *So What: New and Selected Poems, 1971–2005*, translated by Peter Cole, Yahya Hijazi, and Gabriel Levin.

Gratitude as always to friends—especially Carl Dennis, Jeffrey Harrison, Tony Hoagland, and Bernard Horn—who helped with these poems.

I.

Self Portraits

Just Once

Drop the personal, my best friend tells me,
as if, at my age, I ought to know something
beyond the small insights gained from an individual life.
Yet what else do I have? Sent to this planet
just once, briefly, I'm like one of those Mars landers
that crawl along the terrain, sampling what's underfoot.
And it's not encouraging. I'm learning, for example,
that the body slowly wears out—healing, for a time,
unlike a car—but still prone to breakdowns.
And the boat I'm on—trying once more to write,
as I so often have, in the solitude of the cabin—
isn't like the boat in the ad I saw
scudding along, but more like a collection of systems
determined to fail. Yesterday, when Nan
motored over the line to the dinghy, fouling our prop
(my fault, since she wouldn't know to check),
it spoiled the idyll of this little harbor town,
though the bluefish for dinner was fresh and sweet.
Pull the dinghy close when backing up next time!
I know that—have known it for decades—
but I'm forgetful, undermining any small gains
in wisdom. Yet the moving sun   up so early,
still orange, stage-lighting the cabin
with its fiery parallelogram—seems promising.
And more than ever I know such moments
ought to be entered in some ship's log—
along with the breaching of a whale I saw yesterday,
just before sunset, a young one, probably,
but at least the size of my boat, jumping
clear out of the water, as if the sea

vowed to educate me in person—
the sea that refuses to speak
despite so much teeming inside.

Two Walks

The walk I took
with my friend
when he set out a problem
we both knew
neither could solve.

And the walk I took
with my wife
with its little agenda—
four items I'd saved up
to tell her about, including
my walk with my friend.

Meanwhile, the spring
of New England, grudging
and lovely, flooding
the relenting air
with gold light, gold
on the bare trees, and gold
on the bristles of last year's
cornstalks in the dark
earth of the rain-damp field.

Walk, and walk, and walk—
my wife, my friend,
everything orderly and thoughtful
as a Sabbath, a talker
and a listener, a listener
and a teller, the scenery
insisting on perspective,
the crisis good material

once we'd studied it,
chuffing and striding
while the brain

enjoyed its fresh air,
burning all the brighter,
like a flame on top
of the body—or like
a child on its parent's
shoulders—some clouds
flying ahead of us
in the lengthening
and assuaging daylight
of early spring.

The Coyote

If you stripped a dog of its social eagerness,
gave it a loping indifference to human presence
and starved it, you'd have a coyote,
stalking like a shadow among the garbage cans
at the top of Pearl Street, near the Fine Arts Work Center.
We're heading back to our car through a fine mist,
the streetlights haloing amid the black trees,
and we stop, watching him appear and disappear
gaunt as a Giacometti. He's nothing
like a dog bounding into the street.
Does he care if this *is* a street?—or just a hard place
under his paws. Ever since childhood
I've tried to be alert to what people are up to,
but why not see the coyote's point of view?—
how he prefers to ignore them,
following his own track through the darkness.

At the Dentist

I am the father of a disabled son
who is now thirty-seven. Among his problems,
an extraordinary sensitivity to pain.
I accompany him into the treatment room
and can see his open mouth, spotlighted,
bright blood on his teeth.
Even nitrous oxide doesn't help,
though he sees the dentist he saw as a child.
I wish I could alleviate his suffering
with some practical training.
Or else put in my earplugs
so deep grand piano chords
resound in my ears and I swell with beauty
as the music billows inside me . . .
When my son was born
there was a poem the pediatrician liked
and gave out to his patients
to comfort fathers. Could I write
such a poem? A middle-sized graybeard,
with a voice a little on the high side,
trying to speak gently to the world
that needs so much care,
as it floats like a single-celled organism
in a vast bath of darkness . . .
I'd rather think about the old sloop
that I've cared for: after many hours
of scraping and cleaning, we can set forth
with no thoughts of maintenance.
Perfect sailing days when she heels,
then steers herself, and I stand on the bow
beyond the curve of the genoa

to look back at the churning wake
that will never perturb the sea. . . .
Will my son ever be on his own?
Yesterday I heard him
touch typing, about a hundred words a minute,
very loud, on an old typewriter—
some bird, it turns out, trying to find
a home behind one of the shutters.
And in other fantasies he's driving
a city bus, and will have a steady paycheck
and a good pension. As for my country,
it's kinder than you'd think
given all the Social Darwinist rhetoric lately.
For example, it provides him with food stamps,
and gives him a bit extra, too,
paying *him* taxes, just as the dentist
is kind beyond any professional obligation,
and the hygienist too, who modestly states,
"You can hold my hand, and stare
right at me, if you want. I know
I'm not much to look at. . . ."
But she is!   with her brown eyes
behind her tortoiseshell glasses,
meeting his gaze the way the world
tends to meet it, without turning away.

Pathetic, Those Chickadees

Thumb-sized, perched,
a pair of them,
on the weeping cherry near
the hole in the studio wall
covered over by the carpenters
who've been reshingling.
Do those birds feel what I would,
their gray, half-bald
fledgling walled-up now,
a Cask of Amontillado
horror? Or is it mere instinct
that keeps them hovering,
ready to feed? Either way
they remain a curious token:
my wife and I unable to stop
caring for our young, though
they're not young. Our son,
middle-aged, flailing in negative
checking account balance futility,
while the bank piles on fees
preying on the helpless. Of course
we rescue him, unable to stop,
till we're called "enablers."
Oh, little birds, I don't
know the first thing about
how birds feel. I'm the large
irrelevancy at the base
of the tree, staring at the sky
while you wait, perched
on the branches. . . . Only an hour
since their baby's tomb was caulked,

and already their search and rescue operation
seems called off. Now the branches
are silent, or if you want to
put it another way,
still weeping.

Sincerity and Authenticity

When I see that my friend, a poet,
gets slammed by a critic
for writing even a few lines unadorned by metaphor,
seemingly offhand in their prosy variety of vowels,
their appealing chancy rhythms of day-to-day intelligence,

then I feel I ought to give up on poetry,
since the sun of free verse is setting, the star of confession
has sunk below the equator, and here's a hemisphere full of boats
that have never sought the pole star of earnestness,
but are circling instead under rockets
shot from the deck by drunkards with fireworks.

The "common" reader knows sincerity is just "sincerity"—
but still likes to hear the sound of it,
the music of distress, like a melody we long for
in the middle of all that symphonic invention—

the way Dvorˇák wrote a tune in the *New World Symphony*
that really did become a Negro spiritual!—
so beautiful and alarming in its loyal longing—
the way I like my friend to sound,
if only from time to time,
the language of the heart, used carefully,

the way Merce Cunningham used ordinary people
walking across the stage among his dancers,
because not every line in the poem of his dance
had to dance.

The Terrible Memory

After a while, it becomes your friend,
which is useful. "Nothing again can be so terrible."
Well, that's what it tells you:
that you lived through the terror like a fairy tale.

But the terrible memory is also a warning . . .
how one planet can become another,
with three black moons in front of an enormous blue sun.
"Ah, science fiction!"—says the terrible memory,
as if it never happened. You were drawn in
but then the film ended, the credits rolled.

But in the dark, when your thoughts are particularly awful and repetitive,
the terrible memory is happening as if it is no memory at all
but some kind of persistent phenomenon.

Go away, you tell it. This is not the time.
And the terrible memory obeys. It moves backwards through the doorway
as if you are the sovereign. But your sleep is troubled.
What have I forgotten?—you ask.

And soon, like a parent summoned to a child's bed,
it returns to comfort you. *Terrible, terrible,* it soothes,
making a promise to protect you it can never keep.

Hate

Once you have been in a state of hate,
you remember, as though someone threw

a blanket over your head and kidnapped you
away from blond fields the wind strokes,

clamped your head into a vise, and forced you
to keep repeating a single name.

I, personally, never want to go back there.
A one-room apartment overlooking a patio

not far enough down to jump. Hatred
was in me and was all of me, except

for a still small voice of irony, like the chink
of light in a closet, when a child hides in the folds

of wool suits and a bead of light, an ever-brighter
pin-prick, assaults the darkness, just as hate

is assaulted by laughter. That was back
when I hated, I tell myself. It was like

having one leg, one ear, one hand,
and just a piece of a brain, just a piece

of a thought, like a stuck car horn,
so no one could hear himself think

on the blocked road that turned out, finally,
to be wide enough to pass through.

A Little Ode to Television

After the disorder of my days, and in the defeat of my evenings,
I love the quiet, revocable suicide of television,
especially British detective shows, where everyone
is driving cooperatively on the left, but the devoted detective
has broken many rules, and her superior officer
is inevitably impeding the plodding investigation,
while everyone speaks according to region and social class
and the rain tumbles down from the heavy
upholstery of the British sky.

I'm comforted knowing that the improbable murderer
will end up behind bars, or will die being captured, while the detective,
quietly vindicated, will return to her paperwork and her loneliness,
not unlike mine, isolated inside the rain-drenched black umbrella
of her nights. And I feel safe knowing a hundred more episodes are waiting,
each as fateful as the sunset, and shaped by the same conventions
of order and mayhem. And I must never forget
to sing the praises of the music too—the royal
French horns, and the screeching violins of terror
at the spilling of British blood—and how all of it leads
perfectly into sleep.

How Big? (PD)

"This," she says, "you have to see."
She crouches before her refrigerator
and among the photos held up by magnets
(including one of Nan and me)
a strip of black-and-whites that shows
a looming alien head, bowed toward its chest
as if in solemn concentration.

"It"—since they don't want to know
the sex. So one magnet says Aaron
and the other says Charlotte—
our grandchild Aaron/Charlotte!—
and I'm staring at her mass of wavy hair
as she crouches in front of the nebula
of her approaching child, the features
like clouds. She knows about sonograms
from her training as a nurse. "In theory . . ."
She holds her fingers as far apart
as you would to measure out, say,
half a loaf. "And he's a squirmer.
Or she. Must take after Mom.
Not me." Then she's off to work
the graveyard shift at the hospital.

She stands sideways so I can see
the arc of her stomach where it's swimming
in darkness, in silence—all anticipation
and no memory?—while I'm all memory:
the clatter when she dropped her schoolbag,
the angry outbursts, the sobs, the singing,
the escape to the piano, the storm of chords . . .

Walking home, I try to imagine her
stationed in her flowered smock,
on the locked ward, her patients
sleeping, her desk lamp lighting
her reports, her thoughts
blooming, the hallway
before her pinging with silence . . .

It's like waiting for a storm—
a really big one—not even named yet—
one that could last
the rest of her life.

The News

So often the words rise into my throat,
Dad, what should we do about this?

Given the diagnosis, he's the last one I can ask,
since obliviousness is one of the symptoms,

like an atmospheric disturbance, a TV screen
flooded with snow. The books I've read all tell me

his brain is likely to be developing backwards.
Last in, first out. He can explain the wisdom

of Copernicus, versus Galileo, who was rash.
But calls me a paradox—why is my beard gray

if my hair is blond? He recalls our boat trip
to postwar Europe—with cigarettes for currency,

and the poor rabbi onboard—do I remember?—
who kept kosher and had to eat out of cans. . . .

That bemused sympathy must have been there
since childhood. But he's depressed too,

piecing together what's missing, like the tax return
I'm here to help him with. I found him rereading

his report for his twenty-fifth college reunion,
as if to look up who he actually is.

So I felt I should tell him the news about Becky,
my feelings collapsing on me like a building.

And when she called him—"I'm pregnant,"
she'd planned to tell him—he picked up, saying,

"Hello, Becky! Am I talking to one of you,
or two?"—tipped off—and witty, as usual.

Didn't I know Becky would call?
That's me. Panicking he wouldn't know

how to feel—how important the news was—
the way he feels he has to teach me—about the genius

of the alphabet—the Chinese never thought it up!—
and the evolution of language . . . the mixture

of Hebrew and Aramaic spoken on the cross—
Hebrew for *daddy*, Aramaic for *abandoned*.

A Message from My Mother

You may think I watch you constantly now,
the way I'd lifeguard you when you were swimming,
but remember, you've lived longer than I have,
so how can I advise you? Think of me as fading
like a photo on the refrigerator the sun bleaches.
When I do observe you—and my coverage is spotty—
I'm concerned only that you worry too much.
I can tell you from up here, above time,
that it's just the way Chaucer describes it
at the end of *Troilus and Criseyde*. Remember how small
his earthly pains seemed in the light of the stars?
Once you know you have a fate you can relax
in making decisions. And maybe that happens eventually.
Never to me. Now the birds fly through me
effortlessly, as if I'm the air, and the love I felt
has thinned like smoke. I'm glad you can feel it
if I can't—I who once cried for Keats
in the Protestant Cemetery. I cry that way
for myself now when I remember how I swam
floating on my back in the sea and watching
wispy clouds. I'm one of those clouds,
so how can I insist? Do what you will.
The sun is on the water, and the breeze is flying.
Stay in or go out. If you round the point
later this evening you'll see fireworks over the harbor.
Or stay in and don't. Once you've lost it,
you'll know the world was bigger than your life.

II.

Partners

"The River Merchant's Wife"

Back when I first fell in love with Chinese poetry,
and believed my love for my girlfriend would last beyond death,
I read "The River Merchant's Wife"—

a poem so touching it made me want to learn Chinese—
to be able to say so simply some crushing truth
about time and change.

My girlfriend was leaving for college in Ohio,
a long trip down a river that flowed one way,
while I had to stay at home to grow sad,
as the monkeys made sorrowful noises overhead
in the jungle of my adolescence—

sad, but not wise enough to be plainspoken,
nor as uncomplaining as the river merchant's wife,
translated from a language of single syllables,

though the single syllable of love, as I understood it back then,
was stuck in my head like a tiny brass bell
playing its solo in my stupefied mind.

Now perhaps it seems a bit mad—
a young woman's desire to mix her ashes with another's
"forever, and forever, and forever."

But I still know the feeling. The disbelief
all over again at the thought of parting—

from the one I love now, I mean,
she whom I would go to meet anywhere—
even far off Cho-fu-Sa.

To Vocabulary

I wake up between flannel sheets
like a small animal in a pocket
and a) it's sunny, and b)
it's not time to go teach yet,
and c) I feel very clean
(from swimming last night),
and d) there's a feeling between
my legs like a kind of quiet
humming, like a smooth motor—
not desire, or its opposite,
numbness, but the other
opposite, a luxuriating comfort-
ableness, so sex still works
its lubricating contentment
and the word *incorrigible*
returns to me, lost last night
during a brief quarrel.

Why a quarrel? Unimportant,
since it's over, but then
incorrigible was the word I needed,
because it has an overtone
of loving indulgence,
but could only think *intractable*,
or *obdurate*, or *refractory*,
so the argument ended
with something missing.

Until I felt the mischief
of her goodnight kisses,
and her skin smoother than water

with talc floating on it, as though
her buttocks were like drops
that ought to burst
but didn't, liquid inside,
just as her skin foretold,
as if sex were an answer
to all my quibbling.

A Walk to the Spring

"That ring will outlive you," my friend says,
pointing to the gold band I've never taken off
since my wedding decades ago.
Why he's chosen this one object
to make his point, I'm not sure.
He could have pointed to the cement *bassin*
marked "1901" or the rusted, ruined car
with huge fat fenders and running boards
and a tree growing right through its sunroof,
since almost all objects outlive us.
And why I answer, "But I can think!"
I'm not sure, but we're conversing in French,
and Descartes' formula is running through my brain,
along with Pascal's *un roseau pensant.*
My friend, a young widower with many lovers,
says, "Think of the babies conceived in that car."
And the women we pass get comments as well—
"breasts you could get lost in" or "chunky as a tree trunk."
The one who intercepts us, when we reach *la source,*
to tell us she's the owners' daughter
smiles at my friend, as all women do,
an ironic smile of suspicion and attraction,
while she smiles more openly at me—
because of my wedding band or my awkward French?—
as if I'm innocent of the dance of seduction
going on before my eyes. Walking with my friend
is like walking with a cat. He ignores gates,
like this one marked *"privée,"* and sniffs everything.
No wonder this woman's dog wanted to chew him to pieces.
Now it rests in her arms, peaceful and enchanted.

Uncontested

The divorce was uncontested.
One person tried very hard to stay married,
but finally gave up. He was
the faithful type, his mother's name
tattooed on his right shoulder. Was that
the problem, the reason the sad divorce
was uncontested? The other person
was on her way from point A
to point X, Y, or Z, and he was only
point B. Hardly a contest.
She was surveying the far horizon.
He was studying the bottles on the night table
that she was sweeping into a cloth bag
to take with her, that he would miss.

At least there were no children,
so it was a clean, uncontested divorce,
with little or no collateral damage.
No surgery to remove a tattoo.
No home ownership, no haberdashery
or farm to be divided.
For days he could hardly lift his eyes
to the students in his classroom. While she
felt years lighter, and enormously newer,
with no contest between his regret
and her elation. All this
and his mother's death,
like a lesson in acceptance.

When he massages his own shoulder
as he does reflexively now, he's touching

the name of his wonderful mother, whose aggravation
with his father had never resulted in divorce—
divorce that is the uncontested victor over marriage,
the way the flood is champion over the flood plain,
or the fire over the dry fields.

Quintet

When one of the four bridge partners collapses in Andreyev's "The
    Grand Slam,"
and the other three, who have been playing with him every afternoon for
    decades,
realize they don't even know his address, I think of my quintet,
repeating the same music for years, once a month, in the clarinetist's house
through the birth of several generations of Labrador retrievers,
talking about jobs sometimes, much more about dogs, and making yet
    another try at the still-impossible music
(impossible since we're all busy and don't have time to practice).

And what shocks me isn't the death in the story, or the players agreeing
    to glide through the game
without knowing each other very well, or the thought that what makes
    it a story at all
is that death alone can part them, though they hardly "know" each other,
an assumption I thought my quintet would take for granted,
playing Haydn's *Divertimento* (one of our few presentable pieces) in some
    old age home together
if we all live that long. No, it's what the flutist said yesterday,
how she's fed up with the clarinetist's lack of tone,
a distaste that's been building since she's started to play with some other
    groups,
and now thinks that playing with us really isn't a very satisfying musical
    experience.

Now, it's true the clarinetist is very bad, self-taught in middle age,
and it's true that the one time in the last decade she couldn't make it
her replacement made the group feel depressed with longing—all those
    notes we never heard!

But how does one learn to be callous enough to get rid of someone?
Not to think of those squeaks and gasps as just part of the family's noises?

So if we don't divorce the clarinetist, the flutist will leave us,
the way the clarinetist often leaves us when she's reading right through
    repeats and *dal segni*,
and we're stuck with a situation that's like our lives outside of music,
    without music's periodic resolutions.

Still, this may blow over. Lately the clarinetist has been playing louder,
    which improves her tone,
and the flutist, tense from a new job, seems to appreciate the consistency
    of our rules:
how, when voices drop out in confusion, we agree to meet at the double
    bar, take a breath, and play on.

Oxytocin

"A peptide produced in the body during orgasm; when
it is sprayed in the noses of experimental subjects, they
become more trusting and coöperative."
—*The New Yorker*, February 12, 2007

In the evening I drive to my wife's new studio
in town, where she has dinner waiting—
two plump chicken halves from Boston Market,
and sides, and a salad. It's all in plastic,
extemporized but homey, like meeting one's mistress.
I know location does have an effect on her sex drive.
It increases in unfamiliar places, though
the man, of course, is familiar? All evening
we find ourselves touching, even while arguing
over details in the chapbook we're publishing—
her paintings, my poems—or while watching TV,
Grey's Anatomy, which she calls *McDreamy*
after the male lead she thinks is appealing,
through the snow of her thrift-shop set.
Yes, this inconvenience is like dating
as I recall it from ages gone by,
the body uncomfortable, though excited,
on strange furniture. And when it comes time
to make up the bed, I let her do it,
as though I don't belong here, am only visiting
for purposes of renewal, release, the surge
of oxytocin sprayed throughout the body
and the relaxed satiety that follows
before sleep. When I rise the next morning
to move my car from the overnight lot
I am full of trust. The freezing day

will be good, the clouds like puffs of snowbanks
swimming toward the ocean, the dazzling gold
of the tiny sun. I drive westward,
stop at our suburban Y to swim,
then head to our house to read some legal briefs.
One of our union officers is suing another,
and they both appear so ludicrously quarrelsome,
simply in need of love, sweet love.

Married to Me

If she thinks of me as she moves about her brightly lit studio,
she probably imagines me swimming laps at the Y,
not here, in a cornfield, so close to our house, just parked

and staring at storm clouds. They march in like surf
in the late-October dusk, while the wind over the stubble
filters through the thinning trees, as if through tattered sails.

Over the hill there's still sun, the sky's glow tells me.
On the ocean you can see the last possible moment
of light, and watch the darkness come on so gently

you wouldn't know, till you see the stars glinting on the waves.
What must it be like for her, with a husband whose mind
is at sea so often?—who's always been this way,

even as a child crossing to Europe, watching the liner's long wake
form a four-lane highway of marbleized foam
stretching to the horizon from the black steel hull like a headland,

birds darting over it. I'd stare for hours, and the hills
of the waves, made of green glass, obsidian, and sea swirls,
were all folding and folding like a giant's breathing. The sea

cold and miles deep, the world still unformed, like pockets of space,
here before the land crystallized with its rooftops and TV antennas,
and I could hear the hiss of the opaque and fire-swirled wall

at the edge of everything. She'll want to know
I'm somewhere. "At sea" doesn't count. I'll need
to knock on the glass of her studio when I get back.

Once I was on a passage from Boston to the Vineyard,
the weather so rough I couldn't call on my radio. When I landed
she was still angry. Hardly spoke. I wonder

was it for some grief over me? Herself?
Something she wouldn't tell me? The way she won't say much
about whatever overwhelms her while she paints and listens

to her favorite CDs. "Something—" she'll laugh,
amazed. "I was just working, and suddenly these sobs!"
A squall, she'll call it—"then—it was gone."

The Tiny Couple

The tiny couple, under their white, lacy bower,
on the breakfront in my grandparents' parlor
under a bell jar, to keep the dust off—
they were my parents: Dad, a homunculus
in a tuxedo, and Mom, the Thumbelina beside him.
Of course I understood they began that way,
tiny, and knowing nothing, like newborn kittens.
Now they were enormous, and authoritative.
They had been married since the dawn of time,
falling instantly in love on a cruise, and resolving
to create my sister (who seemed a lot of trouble)
and me (a sunny and charming chatterbox),
and had formed a comfortable, unsurprising union,
like a comb and brush. Unless the tiny couple
wasn't them at all. Where were my father's glasses,
my mother's blond hair? Maybe they just represented
marriage, the way my toys represented boats
and airplanes, but couldn't sail or fly,
while the tossed blankets and the sour-sweet smell
of my parents waking up when I opened their door,
or my mother's funny threats at the beach—
"Put down your newspaper, or I'll . . . divorce you!"—
stood for that complicated, living alliance
I'd need more education to understand.
Years later, sure they loved each other,
I still can't completely describe how.
People say each marriage contains a mystery,
but don't we know a good one when we see one?
The little couple from the wedding cake?—who can say
they're not like all of us at the beginning—
dumb and clueless as two toothpicks, rigid

as soldiers vowing never to leave each other's side.
However limited, you have to start somewhere.
As for my parents' sweet exasperated colloquy,
here's how things go, they told me, huge
as gods: you meet, you stand side by side,
frozen but hopeful, and soon you look like a world.

Ashore in Oak Bluffs

The big oaks on the green amid the gingerbread cottages
are shivering and gesturing in the unsettling wind,
    and I'm wondering if the weak link in my anchor chain,

the silvery shackle I used to join it when it snapped
last year in a storm, will hold down there in the harbor
    some miles away. The cottage we're visiting

has a *Wizard of Oz* motif—with tiny Oz figures
half-concealed in the shrubbery. Our friend who owns it
    doesn't care about the story. She's more a conservator

of the previous owner's kitschy taste. And knows
the storm of protest the other cottagers would feel in their hearts
    if she tossed out the figurines, featured

in so many photos. Sometimes she'll find strangers
sitting on the porch, posing. "It's OK," they'll tell her,
    "the owner isn't home." And the wittiest will ask

why the short brick walk leading to the porch isn't yellow.
The Wizard of Oz. The very story that featured in my childhood nightmares
    when I was feverish. With its flying monkeys

and destructive winds. Not like the wind last night,
bathing us in a bugless coolness, as it found its way down the hatch.
    We'd walked from town. And the wind helped us

on the long row from the dock, so the oars dipped gently
into the moonlit current. This must be happiness, I thought,
    when Nan reached over to show me the screen

of her camera, and I saw my face, lit by the strobe light,
with an extraordinary smile of gleeful surprise. Because everything
    was helping: the wind, the current, Nan pointing the way

to the anchored boat with its little lantern on its boom.
And then that soothing sleep. Nightmareless. Even the dawn
    fishing boats passing slowly, courteously, making only

the smallest wake. Such happiness. Like the opening
of a movie, before any violence. Or like the ending of a dream
    when the same breeze hushes the thought

that the whole island's only temporary. Can you see me,
the tiny figure in the tourists' photos? I'm the one on the porch
    who seems so distracted, listening

to what the oaks are telling me.

✓The Afterlife (PD)

There's a lot of light in her apartment,
falling on the rented hospital bed.
I've been told the dying like to be held,
so, though we're just friends, I make myself
hold her hand, as if the conversation is final,
matters more than others, though most have mattered.

She's seen a couple of rabbis, who were helpful.
It seems there are Jewish angels. (Why argue?)
And she likes the story I brought her,
"The Death of Ivan Ilych," how before the end
he learns so much nobody knows about,
except the reader.

"So many faces," she says of the people who came
for the songfest yesterday evening, over a hundred
crowded into this little place. "Each face a flower.
Each face . . ." and here she pauses
(the medicines are affecting her word retrieval?)
"so full of memories."

It all makes a strange image in my head:
faces that aren't faces, but wide open,
as if she's discovering that she's lived
everything they have—centuries
more than she thought.

"Our life in others," I remind her,
(citing Pasternak,) "that is our immortality."
But she knows that doesn't go far enough.

I'm glad she's thinking of her own afterlife,
since not being alive is, apparently, unthinkable
on the brink of it happening, a kind of shallowness
to imagine it's merely like going to sleep,
though lately her dreams have been so vivid:
an all-night argument with her sister about a dog,
over what color it should be, white or black.

Outside the weather appears to be changeable.
I'm dying to go out there, on the small terrace.

"Go out on the terrace," she says, "before you leave.
The view is wonderful."

III.

Offshore

Imagining Uruguay

Since few people know exactly where it is
I doubt anyone will attack it
or its small navy, mostly river boats
flying a flag almost no one would recognize.

Its history, too, is a mystery
or, one should say, undramatic,
with everyone voting on everything
from speed limits to the portraits on money—

and who *are* those men? They are the writers
no one's read, but who are dear to their country.

What a country! Sitting on a bench in a park
along the vast and mostly traffic-free river
studded with green islands without houses,
I feel I have come to a country on the other side of death,
a country too calm to be dreamt of.

The police stroll the town in immaculate white shirts
discussing philosophy, I suppose, since where are the crimes?
No philosophers without jobs in this country.
This country is waiting for events, not swept up in them.
If you want events, you must cross the river.

This is the country of bedroom slippers.
This is the republic of naps. These are the roads
that lead inland to fields of endless grasses.
This is the river so broad it becomes the sea without fanfare.
These are the tame dogs without collars.
These are the winds of peace that carry no sound with them.
These are the birds that sing without prophecy.

Flight from Cyprus

I sleep the way my father did toward the end,
slack-jawed, as if amazed by something so much
he looked dead. When I wake I shut my mouth,
but I'm sure the flight crew has already seen me,
and the passengers hiking back to the lavatories.
A spattering of islands in the Aegean below,
like droplets of cement on the blue stone floor
of the sea, a line of foam along the cliffs
on their windward sides. And all around me
Greek. No longer Hebrew—with words
that pop out at me from childhood—
ever since we changed planes in Cyprus,
another divided country. If I knew
more islands, I'd know who sent soldiers
to Troy with Agamemnon. Few of them
like my father: circumspect and reasonable.
Each land should have such fathers. A cool
blue, that blue and reasonable sea
that doesn't need boundaries. And on it,
island after island, obdurate and stony
as Jerusalem, where my friend's son,
glaring with passion, described his land
as if the Bible were a deed. And these days
his father sounds so much like mine—
wry, practical, and smart. "Not much to be done,"
my friend will shrug. As my father used to,
serene now where the gods live, while below
tiny ships ply the ancient sea like matchsticks
with white furry tails. If I were leaving the earth
I'd say goodbye from up here, where it's so blue
and reasonable. But here's another island,

ragged as a birthmark, stony and eternal.
And here's a small one, shaped like a comma,
as if the land has been writing on the sea—
the sea that says *everyone's* or *no one's*
while the land says *mine* and *mine* and *mine*.

Reading Taha by Lamplight

And so
it has taken me
all of sixty years
to understand . . .
—Taha Muhammad Ali

Taha, I'm reading your poems by lamplight—
a kind of miner's lantern, that is, that I strap to my forehead
to spare the house batteries on my boat—
and I feel like a miner searching for a tunnel
to sun-struck Nazareth,
to the corner near the church
where you keep your souvenir shop.

Poet of absent villages,
of childhood memories, of places
evaporating like clouds—I apologize
that my relatives banished yours—
their bitterness and hope displacing yours.
Forgive me for putting it that way.

We did not weep
when we were leaving—
for we had neither
time nor tears,
and there was no farewell.
We did not know
at the moment of parting
that it was a parting,
so where would our weeping
have come from?

That's you, exiled
when you were just a boy,
while outside the cabin, as it always does,
the sea scribbles its thoughts,
and then forgets them.

But you can't forget.
This land is a traitor
and can't be trusted.
This land doesn't remember love.
This land is a whore . . .
rests its head along the usurper's thigh . . .

Poet of remembering,
yesterday I saw a whale breach,
hurling its body clear out of the water,
to salute the sun.
It seemed far off—small—
though it was the size of a small schooner.

And it made me think, Taha,
how much room there might be
if we end up sharing the earth someday,
the way fish share the ocean—
so much room to spare,
so much emptiness
between tiny flares of animate life.

Oaxaca

The last time I was here
a man who spent his working life
in a men's room, an attendant
in a white jacket at some
five-star hotel, showed me how
to clean my glasses. He watched
as I washed them at the sink,
as I pulled out my shirttail to try to dry them,
and proffered some ordinary tissue
and mimed what I should do.
So that's what I've continued to do—
clean my glasses with toilet tissue.
I guess the rich live here like children,
instructed by their servants. Or the poor
are inclined to kindness. Or else they
consider the rich their children
as well as their masters, helpless
and essential, with needs to meet,
or everything would whirl off
into revolution. Otherwise life
goes on brightly colored under the sun.
Who are the dancers up on the stage
at the folk dance festival? Who
made their costumes? Who pays them?
Are they teachers from the local high school
earning a little extra on Friday nights?
Or do they stand all day in a cage
at a nearby bank? Or carry crates
of soda bottles to a Coca-Cola truck?
Whirling in their feathers and ribbons
they can't be working. They must be

dancing for the reason anyone dances—
the music goes right through their bones,
their boots thundering on the drum of the stage.

The Blessing of the Poodles

It says clearly, in Spanish: No animals
allowed inside the church. But the tour guide
lets a woman bring along her dog,
a Standard Poodle, quiet, docile,
soft curls like a child's. He tells her
he owns one himself. "One day a year,"
he says, "is set aside to bless the poodles."
Something like the blessing of the fishing fleet
in Provincetown? But not really,
since what risks do these poodles run?

Anyway, this is a Mexican church—
you can pin a *milagro* to a saint who favors you,
perhaps a little replica of your arthritic knee,
and hope for relief. Do they bless burros too?—
those long processions at night, like apparitions,
heavy bags of compost balanced on their backs,
their heads bowed, accepting labor,
poorly compensated, unending labor,
the way their silent masters do, those men
in the shadows beneath their sombreros?

In my diffuse, liberal religion
God is everywhere, like radio waves,
and just as invisible. But social justice?
Redistributing capital? That's up to us!
The guide tells us about a local priest
who painted a mural somewhere in the sacristy
that features Lenin and Trotsky as heroes—
a kind of backup team for the saints?

I guess he was running out of patience.
Still, I hope he didn't lose faith in a god
who knew the earth, yet believed in the meek—
who took the time to bless the poodles and the fishermen—
not the one beaming cloud-rays from the ceiling,
but this one down here, carved on a lintel
the beggars wait beneath, expressionless—
the one crowned with thorns, riding a burro.

House of Refuge

I'm trying to imagine what the little girls are imagining,
the toddler deep in the dream of being transported here
during a freak October snowstorm, carried
into the rescue boat of our house. It's fiercely warm
in our kitchen, but her mother's round breast
is like a planet she can't bear to leave.
How we laugh, then, when this little one
pulls away from the nipple to shout "Stupid idiot!"
The older one has a meltdown. She will be late for school.
The hostile monster monkeys will laugh.
Back at their cold, darkened house,
why is their powerful garage door crippled?
Or their dark freezer packed with rock-hard meat
festering like a secret they'd hoped to keep?
As for me, I'm strangely happy!
I don't mind the baby wipes in the bathroom,
or the chorus line of Mexican figurines across the piano keys.

At the end of the driveway, the sweet gum I planted
for its shape like a candle flame, for its orange-and-bruise-colored
star-shaped leaves, has a broken limb or two.
It's as if a plaster ceiling has fallen down in a comedy,
the characters blowing dust out of their mouths.
All over town "cherry pickers" reach up into the leaf-laden branches,
as if there were a kind of harvest to be picked
in this unplanned scrambling of households.

The snow mounds in the warm sunshine
remind me of troglodyte houses in Cappadocia
where everything's rounded like drifts, but of amber rock,
reliable shelters in an earthquake. And of my sister,

stuck there for months, living out of cardboard cartons,
in a hotel where the workers are housed on the roof in huts.
Judy! Judy! they would call down to her.
Have you any aspirin? She answered them in Turkish,
and climbed up several flights to bring them some.
How could I continue to worry about her after that?

What the Pig Meant

Yesterday I lost the word *pigment*.
The colored powders were all there
in my head. I could feel the thing's
existence, but the word wouldn't come. . . .
Today I woke up thinking
Was that what the pig meant?—
my mind fastening onto *pig meant*
like an orange life jacket should it threaten
to sink again. And what happens
when I lose more words? Or years?
Twice I visited Provence in May
during this millennium. But which was the year
we walked in the woods near Rousillon,
the cliffs red as the planet Mars? Cliffs
full of pigment. Already I'm losing streets.
Losing towns. Losing "The art of losing. . . ."
Two months since the hospital, and I can't remember
my medicines. (With the names of alien princes
in space movies. *We will obey you, Prince Levaquin.*)
Back on the planet, with my memory redacted,
with little faith I tell myself, *Suck it up.*
Remember what the pig really meant—
the devouring pig.

Walter at the Wheel

When he sails into the harbor
and I compare our boats, his and mine,
I understand he's Walter Cronkite
and I'm not—his a mass of white
with two tall masts, like the broadcast antennae
that reach millions in large cities—
as his face did, his grave, gravelly voice—
billions across the planet. They've said he turned the tide
against the Vietnam war. And retired to the Vineyard,
owner of a large, gleaming yacht
that will only stop briefly at our boat basin
like the visitation of a dream, a cloud
of sail among the little handkerchief
sails of smaller boats like mine.
And I understand that I was part of the mass
of "mass media" that trusted him
to pronounce, "And that's the way it was."
The dockmaster says Walter's ninety-one
and "can hardly get out of his own way,"
though he likes to sit at the wheel
and let his boat carry him around the globe,
the way his fame carried him. Part of history,
like *Old Ironsides* or the *Mayflower*.
My boat is an incidental speck of sail
in a landscape by Benson or Tarbell,
who painted the waters of New England
a century ago. Mine is one mast
in a sea of masts, helping the landscape
complete itself, the way my little head
was a speck, a pixel in the war protest photos
four years before the tide turned
and Walter finally caught on.

Watch Battery

Who knows if my father ever thought
what Montaigne's father did: That every city
should have a place where people in need
could go to meet. How somewhere
a man is starving, and another with a surplus
would grieve if he only knew, and offer the man
a modest but reasonable living. That giving man
could have been my father. Not grieving, perhaps,
but regretful he couldn't be of more help—
a man you could trust to fix things.

Like the man who helped the watchmaker
fix my watch. How, when he couldn't decide
how to loosen the clasp that holds in the battery,
itself no bigger than a small coin,
without breaking it, he turned to someone
more experienced—a Dutchman, actually,
who seemed happy to demonstrate this very skill,
and upload it to YouTube. Demonstrate it
with a camera in his lap, so we could see his two hands
familiarly, competently, and rapidly
opening the watch to replace the battery,
the way a father would automatically retie his son's shoe.

And there was also his calm voice with its accent,
like the woodcarver's in *Pinocchio*,
telling the confused and despairing who were ready
to lose patience and snap the band holding the battery
and ruin the watch—the watch that could keep running—
how to prolong its life by exercising patience,
the very quality my dad had in abundance,

that quality I always loved him for, of solving the problem
without getting exasperated. Though it's unfair
he didn't have parents like that himself.
Or that—when the amount of pain rose to be greater
than any pleasure he'd be able to feel—
the little watch-sized defibrillator near his heart
wouldn't simply stop, and let him go.

Lunch at the Brew Moon

They've closed the cafeteria for the holidays so I'm going
to the Brew Moon with some of my post-post-graduates.
Barbara, in her seventies, missed the last few classes

because she was in India. On the brick sidewalks of Cambridge,
in the biting wind off the December ocean,
under a bitter blue sky, she describes the beggars,

naked children pointing to their mouths. Or the pyre
for a young man—there in the smoke of bodies along the Ganges—
his terrified wife dragged toward the flames by her in-laws.

And at lunch, once our sandwiches come, Catherine
describes the family she works for as a nanny,
the child hugged by his mother before she leaves for the airport

ignoring her—even as he's being held—because
he's spotted Baker, the dog Catherine goes everywhere with.
This child's eleven winter coats. His fourteen pairs of sneakers.

His iPad. Though he does not yet know
his right hand from his left. A different kind of neglect
from that in Catherine's childhood, since a child

as smart and sweet as Catherine, we're told,
was beaten. "Here," said Catherine's mother. "Kill yourself.
Just take this knife and do it—if you're so miserable."

So, of course, a number of times Catherine tried,
though not lately. Lately she's been writing stories
and working on her doctorate. Adria and I

spill onto her salad plate many of our french fries.
It's hard to know at which point to cry,
and when to laugh. It's a mixed-genre lunch.

Like the play across the street, Shakespeare's notorious *Merchant*,
where Shylock, tightfisted, vengeful, spat-upon,
is instructed in the ways of mercy by beautiful Portia,

so rich and treasured. Portia would probably raise her children
like the woman Catherine works for. We laugh.
But Barbara's mind keeps going back to her friend in New Delhi

who keeps a stack of two-rupee notes on his dashboard, and only gives
to beggars who are blind or roll around on wheels, not to the able-bodied—
there're simply too many, crowding up to the car at every crossroad.

In Response to My Fear
That I'll Receive Another Call
from the Yacht Salesman

He is chuckling on another continent,
as if inviting me to come over there
where they live by different rules.
Oh, quintessence of uselessness,
oh sailboat! He is telling me
how a boat with a retracting keel,
self-tacking jib reaching 30° into the wind
will allow me to sail, not motor, out of the harbor,
and change my life. I'm bewildered.
I see the workers in his small English town
standing despondently in a vast hangar
waiting for the word to start building.
Maybe a boat with a blue hull.
And then I see my family staring at me
as if they don't know me. Or those
in my study group who do know
that it's not in acquiring things, but in acts of the spirit
that we gain meaning. Or the cormorants
down there in Blackfish Creek crying,
"We're waiting! We'd just as lief shit on a yacht as on a scow."
And lastly my parents: "We left you a legacy,
now it's up to you to decide if you're a fool."
This boat built to travel all the oceans of the world . . .
I tell them, it's built to Class A offshore specifications.
"Do you want to go offshore?"
my dead mother asks sadly. And my father, as if alive,
shrugs at all this silliness, valuing

neither boats nor money, but only peace.
But haven't I earned the right
to give myself a parting gift from the world?
"No fool like an old fool," someone says.
I hope it's not my wife. A landlubber, basically,
who in screeching winds likes to duck down the companionway
and spread out her charcoal and oil pastels on the cabin table
to get on with her work—drawings that include
levitating sailboats, symbols
for the antic role my moodiness plays
in the otherwise sheltering harbor of her life?
He's willing, says the salesman, to throw in a bow thruster,
the autopilot, and even a canvas dodger,
and ship the boat over for free in return for exhibiting it
at the Newport Boat Show next September.
A boat built to last longer than a man.
A fact I'll appreciate in the September storms off Newport,
when that heavy lifting keel with its seven-foot draft
will reach deep into the sea with its sturdy hand
and save my life. "Well worth the price,"
I say to my wife, who won't be too sure,
though I suppose she'll be glad to have me back
from the storm of my own indecision,
once I decide to let the beautiful sailboat
drift away, and tell the salesman
no, fool that I am.

IV.

What Now?

My Happiness

You wander into my thought,
my happiness, the way the deer
wander through the yard these days,
very relaxed, with no thought of being hunted,
browsing the bushes near the driveway
like people at the refreshment table of an art opening. . . .

That's how you come over me—
not with a burst of wings,
but with that slow, presumptuous air of entitlement,
as if you don't care if I want to be happy,
or what kind of happiness I want.

I could be listening to music,
and notice that behind me
Abigail is dancing—
or doing what she thinks
is dancing—
with her baby arms and feet . . .

And I tell myself this isn't glory
as described in the book I'm reading
where the hero has an insatiable hunger.

No one can help but find this embarrassing—
the way you stroll into one's mind so quietly.

But that's how I recognize you,
my happiness, so furtive, so insouciant,
the way you insist you belong in me

via eminent domain, with no respect
for my sad moods. . . .

Suddenly you're there, like the deer.

And sometimes, perversely,
when I come home after dark,
and see the little herd
chewing on our bushes,
I switch on my high beams
and drive right at them,
till I reach an unspoken boundary
the animal gods must have set,
and they become a forest
of legs and knees
scrambling into the night. . . .

That's how quickly you can flee,
my happiness.

Landlocked (PD

What am I doing, trudging around Natick, Massachusetts,
so archetypal in its split-level, clapboard ordinariness,
one house after another like a crowd gathered haphazardly
at an accident site? And why explore the deafening
blandness of the little streets with fenced-in yards,
where day after day—iPod loaded with arias—
Ti prego, rubami il cuore!—I wheel the baby, who will not quiet
unless she's rolling along through a landscape, however dull,
a child who will grow up some day with the sole ambition
of leaving home. And why keep pretending
the sunlight gives the brick walls a ruddy, Hopperesque gravitas?
It's a dullness that approaches yoga, a meditation,
a boredom so exquisite it's like nonbeing,
from which even the faint fanfare of cobalt blue shutters
can't wake me—sleep-laden, like a boat covered with a tarp—
though here I am, navigating the seismic faults of the sidewalk
with the sidetracked stroller, in a pebble-strewn jiggling
the baby seems to need for her peace. Ah, this do-nothing
self-abnegation of walking the streets of Natick, Massachusetts,
and its neighborhoods—as if life has hardly emerged yet from sleep,
that first sleep, and—like an infant struggling to turn over—
the soul wants to buy a ticket to anywhere
that's out of town, like Venice, say, where the lacy façades
weep into the tarnlike byways and boulevards,
and there's a music of world-weary, self-extinguishing tragedy
to fight with the sun-spangles on the water.

The Blue Boat

If the boat is ugly, but the bay is beautiful,
is the sail a good one? And if the other boats
are beautiful, but their hulls and sails are stenciled with ads,
is the weather still beautiful if the winds are light?
And if the winds are steady enough to take us out of the *calanque*,
tacking from deep inside its high cliffs,
and out across the bay to the base of the mountain,
then back to the cliff, could the cave look
like the mouth of a giant with tonsils showing?
And if the boom hits me in the head, but I'm carrying
aspirin? And if the back of the boat starts leaking
while the front of the boat is automatically bailing?
And if the "president" of the club, who rented us the boat,
offers us white wine grown here in Cassis
when we return, and we spend an hour talking,
is that part of the experience?
And does experience matter more than pleasure?
And is pleasure better than peace? I've nothing
but peace today—and sore bones—
sitting alone in my apartment in Aix
without any phone. My head's stopped hurting.
I'm completely free, but is that better
than assigning myself some task? For example,
editing the photos from yesterday? Here is the boat
the spiders had been living in till we cleaned it.
And here is the foot of water sloshing in the bottom
when we still couldn't stop the leak in the stern.
And these are the huge swirling speckled cliffs
you can't see from the land. And here's me
beneath the shade of my straw hat,

pale as a mushroom dragged out of its cellar,
looking like a scholar who thinks everything's in books,
seduced by a blue boat, and the sea.

When My Book Group Reconvened after So Many Years

We decided to reread Horace. Once again I wished
I'd studied Latin, the language my mother taught
in high school. Sometimes she'd tutor her students
right in our living room. Such complex grammar!
One person, I thought, conversant with a dead language
per family seemed enough.

So now I'm struggling to figure out what the poet means
when he speaks of those who have become shades,
prisoners of Hades. Does he believe in that dark realm,
or just in darkness?

I do know what he means by the dark shadows
he sees under every bright thing, and by the seasons
rolling by. I imagine my mother thought of that
when she wrote about her dream: the earth
turning ever more quickly, and—despite my father
gripping her hand—hurling her off.
Her best poem. Short, but it captured the terror
of dying too young,
only a few years older than Horace.

Carpe diem, quam minimum credula posteram—
which means: enjoy this time to discuss Horace!—
and each one who attends, so familiar and dear—
the very sound of their voices!—since anyone might be absent
from the next meeting, or never come again.

There's no way to keep on meeting indefinitely.
No way to meet down below either, where Horace imagines
the great poets of Greece will be holding a forum. . . .

No forum either. Though I'd like to think
my mother would be there—
waiting for her turn to greet Horace
fluently in his mother tongue.

In November

When my daughter calls
and I can hear her baby
crying in the back seat
and she asks, "Dad, would you mind if I stop by
for a quick diaper change and feeding?"—

I'm so glad I picked up the phone,
glad I hadn't set off on my walk,
and quite soon I see her car rolling into the driveway,
and the baby is stretching open her little mouth
and wailing, as babies do—
so enraged not to be able to speak,
not even to be able to think this or that is wrong
except that the whole universe is wrong.

And when they're settled in the little bedroom off the kitchen,
and the baby is sucking noisily,
and then, contented once more,
rolling both eyes, not always in the same direction—
mother and baby in the bedroom
where my daughter herself was once diapered and fed—

I feel so thankful for never having strayed very far
into the wide world, never having served
in the foreign wars of my time, and grief for fathers
who do, the ones swaddled in flags—
maybe because yesterday was Veterans Day,
and though she says she's never done this before,
my daughter tells me she called up a soldier's family she knew
just to say she'd been thinking of them, just hoping
the war we have now will end soon.

And the thin November light is straining through the window curtains
we've never changed,
and I feel thankful for my years right here in this house
the way I imagine a tree might feel thankful
if it were ever given an opportunity to roam around the world—

how it might say, "So good of you, but no thank you,
where would the birds be without me here?—
the ones that fly back unpredictably
to perch in my thinning hair,
this and every November."

The Reason for the Child

I.

I watched as a child sang to her dolls
in a garden restaurant near La Caume,

arranged them so they embraced,
mixed their doll hair together.

As her mother and father dined,
and her dog looked on, she played

under the table. And the song
I couldn't translate, but its words—

simple, logically rhymed—
must have drawn on what was known

to the child. *My parents*
love me. Our dog loves

us all. I crouch here
with my dolls who are my friends

and love each other as much as me. . . .

II.

The land's been tilled at high cost.
The ruled wheat fields. The extravagant

streaks of red in fields overgrown
with poppies. The bedrolls of hay

burning into fragrance beneath
the brassy hills and the blue

of the heavens—as if the child imagined
a sky wearing huge blue robes,

and a kind parent to present
each thing to her as a gift.

III.

It's not disprovable. No one
can understand if love exists

or only seems to. But say it's belief,
and nothing has a final cause,

then tell me the reason for the child—
for the rest of the earth, for that matter,

left dour and unpraised
without her song.

The Bad Singers
of San Miguel de Allende

While the two singers are strumming their guitars
right behind my head—so close, if I turn
I'll be staring right at their fingers,
right into the hole beneath the strings—
my eyes meet a girl's at the next table,
a rosy-cheeked blond kid, maybe fourteen,
who also clearly thinks the singing is terrible,
whatever it's saying about love, or longing,
the strings of the guitars out of tune
with each other, the man's voice
sliding off the notes, the woman's
sliding even farther. I can only infer
the singer is beautiful, since her voice isn't.
Now I see her. She's not glamorous:
nut brown, round-cheeked like a healthy baby.
She's collecting coins from the relieved patrons,
who feel free, at last, to resume their conversations.
My wife and I talk of the things we talk about
as the years go by. Probably not what the singers
have been singing of. The fire
in the restaurant stove burns brightly.
The singers in their night-blue jackets
are taking their passionate bad singing
back onto the cold cobbled streets,
moving down the block to the next venue
where they're welcomed into a brightly lit doorway.
And when it's time for us to head out too,
I see the blond girl—cheeks flushed
from the warmth of the stove—and pause at her table.

"The singing was the highpoint, no?" She laughs.
Her whole family laughs. My exit line!
But why such a need to be remembered?
Tell me that, oh bad singers!

The Rowboat, The Girl, The Light

Today the pool is pierced
by sunlight, and there's a girl
in my lane, her flesh lit
by reflected light from below
to a subaqueous brightness
the way the water in our boathouse
(demolished long ago)
shone in our faces.
We would lean over to see the striped
shadowy fish, their sides
glinting like belt buckles
or dimes, and the wood
smelled ancient and dry,
and probably the dock
creaked, as my rowboat
thumped against it,
the boat's floor resounding
like a drum when we stamped.

Unsinkable because of
compartments under the seat
like little ovens, so I could
go out alone, provided
I stayed in the cove, our point
in the star-shaped lake,
and hewed close to the shore
I wouldn't have wanted to leave
anyway, because she lived there—
an unfathomably pretty girl,
like the Queen of Heaven.

On the best days she would hail me
from her landing, but once
she jumped in, and swam to me,
her white body dripping
as she clambered aboard.
Then everything smelled of pine.
I think that's how desire felt then—
like an odor, the pines
that covered the hillside
above her house.

Desire these days feels like desire
for everything. The air
I strain to breathe, the white
clouds rumbling across
the blue outside the pool's
picture windows, and the little
pinpricks of light
on people's fenders
as the traffic passes.

Alive! Alive! each stroke
like the clenching of the heart.

Love Poem

The sail is so vast when it's laid out on the driveway.
I stake it with a screwdriver through the shackle
at the tack to stretch it smooth,
pulling on the head and clew. Now it's smooth
as a night's worth of new snow.

My wife, my partner, has been torn from her busy day.
We face each other across the sail's foot
and with my right hand and her left hand
(I'm right-handed, she's left-handed)
we pull an arm's length of the sail
down over itself, then do this again,
keeping my left hand and her right hand
inside the latest fold, and drawing our other hand,
her left hand and my right hand, toward the foot.

Each fold is easier since the sail grows narrower
near the top. Then we fold toward each other,
and I wrap my arms around it, while she holds the bag's mouth open,
the gray bag that will cover it through the winter.
Then I thank her. And the driveway is visible again
as it is in spring, when all the snow has melted.

Fame

I notice a gaggle of men surrounding a blonde;
Nan notices—with her artist's eye
and her absolute recall for faces—Claire Danes.
On this barren Saturday in Chelsea,
the sidewalks almost empty, the galleries closed,
the men seem self-satisfied, excited—
the younger ones especially seem frenetically delighted
to surround her with a cloud of adoration,
as if she were the Virgin Mary in a mural with cherubs.

I'd be glad to join them, if I weren't so inhibited.
"We could walk around the block," Nan suggests,
"without seeming to follow her." But no,
"I hate it when people gawk at *me*," I tell her—
a running joke we have between us:
Nan, who would adore fame, and I
who also would adore fame but can't admit it.

I'd love to have some verses of mine on a railing
overlooking the water. Have you seen the railing
with a quote from Whitman and a quote from O'Hara?—
the one about wanting a record store nearby
as a sign people don't completely regret life.
There *are* no more record stores.
Now kids will be asked to look up "record store" in the dictionary,
just as they'll need to look up "mettlesome"
so they can understand Whitman's part of the railing.

Down near 14th near Prince Lumber
I declare to Nan that I *am* Prince Lumber
come to carry her off to my family lumberyard

and seduce her with the clean scent of sawdust!
But still, I'm not goofy enough to stalk Claire Danes
who at fifteen played Angela
in the short-lived TV series, *My So-Called Life*—
who seemed to have such brilliant thoughts back then—
thoughts that were impossible to reveal, let alone
cast in metal. First she'd pout, then she'd beam,
a champion of feeling versus everything else.

Passionate and mettlesome—that's what Whitman called the city.
And indeed my heart turns molten at the thought of Claire Danes
moving along the Manhattan streets in her sacred mist—
she who will always be fifteen,
just starting to catch on to things,
a stand-in for myself, I guess, though prettier.

To Teaching

Now that I'm about to retire
I wonder if I'll miss you—you, my opportunity
to converse seriously with the young.

And what will I be like without you?
Will I make myself my own student?
Or will I try you out on other old ones,
silver heads bent over a text together. . . .

You are much of what I admired years ago in Kenneth Koch
when he was up in front of our class, thinking about the surprises
of, say, similes in the *Iliad*, and he was excited, talking,
as if every word were new just as it was being uttered,
bubbling out of a certain area of the cerebral cortex
I think of as an overdeveloped muscle for doing you.

I have almost felt religious while in the midst of you,
or when meeting those students who've come back after decades
and swear they've been changed for the better. . . .
Not by me! But by you, sweet vocation!

They say no one can be taught to do you, which may seem odd to you,
but sometimes you may be inside a person from the start—
like a passion for giving traffic directions.

Remember the time I was being mugged in Riverside Park
by a scared guy who had been asking me questions about my camera—
a German one, I was glad to explain to him, and not all that expensive—
and you took over, and you tried to make him consider
Methadone? And he stopped the mugging,
became your student for the moment, and simply took my cash,

though he did leave me enough for bus fare?
Thank you for showing me that even he
was a child inside, who wanted to be approved of,
to have his name written on the blackboard with stars—
and once it was, to succumb to your spell.

FOR THE MEMORY OF KENNETH KOCH

How to Improvise

Sometimes your fingers land on a note you don't expect—
a sudden key change, or a chord so muddled
there's not even a name for it—
and you're charged with making the best of it.

If in doubt, repeat a mistake
until it doesn't sound like one,
the way Stravinsky liked to repeat an odd hunch of notes
till it rewired our brains.

But then comes a brain-dead moment
when you have no idea what the rest of the thought should be
but feel too embarrassed to go back to the same theme,
so you let your fingers fall on the keys.
Maybe *they* have an idea you can tumble around?

And at times you'll feel someone has posed a question
that will totally flummox you, since you have arrived
at that dangerous moment when the thread of the piece
is about to snap into silence, and there is a prayerful quiet within you
as if your heart has actually stopped nowhere near a defibrillator. . . .

No, here comes one, and you're ticking again,
and on goes the music toward its formal
if unforeseen conclusion, the tonic note you know
you have to wend your way toward
no matter how many others you might think of to delay
the unquestionable end.

A Summer Afternoon

I'm in the kiddy pool with Abigail,
who seems sleep-deprived, and far too quiet,
surveying the panorama—big kids
shrieking and leaping—with her little frown,
as if she's asking what all this is for,
so much energy spent jumping in
just to hoist oneself out and jump again.
Why don't I play with her?—summon up some
vitality, instead of becoming
pensive myself, feeling unproductive,
and noting how most other "peak" moments
also leave me empty? Or *am* I bored?
Isn't she more companionable when
she's sad? I'll pretend to be sitting with her
on a rock by the sea—a place that helps
with broad and brooding philosophical
thoughts. So what is the nature of this gift,
I would ask, of a summer afternoon?
What will she say? Zoe, older, wants to
show me how well she can stand on her head.
I get in the water too, to show her
how long I can, keeping my feet aloft,
a kind of flirting. Then they both go home
with our daughter, while I end up eating
at Shanghai Gardens. *Enjoy the moment!*
my cookie tells me. Don't brood on how you
feel confused by sadness and happiness
on an afternoon you wished engaged you
more! Don't think quite so much. Were you confused
when the girls dashed away from you, aiming
to drown each other in the deep end? Nope.

Your mind was concentrated then. Like theirs.
Hours of boredom, enlivened by moments
of terror. Just what people say about
sailing. And the feeling beneath it all—
I don't mean the momentary gliding
liftoff into bliss, nor the overcast
ennui, but something so general and
world-encompassing it's more like the sea
running under your keel—I'm still hoping
to find a name for. If it isn't joy.

The Light

I'm dealing with a chain of probabilities
only, coasting across the bay at night
under the swaying stars. I check the compass
regularly, but there's no way to know
if I can beat the current rounding the point.
I'll have to let the boat tell me
when I get there, and trust to experience
or luck. It's exciting and also relaxing
not to know. I'm practicing trust
in myself and my Bermuda sloop,
especially since I can't know anyway
if the cloud that begins to blot the stars
might be fog, or a storm, or
just a bit of haziness. Not all voyages
need the stars for navigation,
but I'm practicing trust in the heavens too,
or at least a neutral attitude
about disaster, assuming the stars
favor me just as often as they don't,
assuming the next buoy should
appear two points to starboard
if the night stays clear—one flash
every four seconds—crossing the bay
and meant for me.

The Four Lakes Prize in Poetry

Series Editor
Ronald Wallace

Sponsored by
the University of Wisconsin–Madison Department of English

The Four Lakes Prize in Poetry is given periodically to one new book of poetry submitted by a past winner of either the Brittingham Prize in Poetry or the Felix Pollak Prize in Poetry and is selected by an editorial board comprised of poets in the University of Wisconsin's creative writing program. Submissions to the Brittingham and Pollak competitions by previous winners are automatically considered for the Four Lakes Prize. With this prize the University of Wisconsin Press will continue to welcome poets new to the series through its annual competition, while supporting the winners' further development by publishing new works.

For more information, visit creativewriting.wisc.edu/submit.html or uwpress.wisc.edu/series/four-lakes.html